β

O

COMETS, METEORS, AND ASTEROIDS
Voyagers of the Solar System

by Ellen Lawrence

Consultants:

Suzy Gazlay, MA
Recipient, Presidential Award for Excellence in Science Teaching

Kevin Yates
Fellow of the Royal Astronomical Society

Published in 2014 by Ruby Tuesday Books Ltd.

Copyright © 2014 Ruby Tuesday Books Ltd.

Editor: Mark J. Sachner
Designer: Emma Randall

Photo Credits:
European Space Agency: 20–21; NASA: Cover, 6–7,
8, 10–11, 13, 14, 15 (bottom left), 19 (top), 19 (bottom
right); Public domain: 4–5, 15 (bottom right), 16,
19 (bottom left); Ruby Tuesday Books: 9, 12, 22;
Shutterstock: Cover, 17, 18; Superstock: 15 (top).

Library of Congress Control Number: 2013939990

ISBN 978-1-909673-22-9

Printed and published in the United States of America

For further information including rights and
permissions requests, please contact our Customer
Service Department at 877-337-8577.

Contents

Words shown in **bold** in the text are explained in the glossary.

A Bright Light in the Sky

Imagine that you're out walking at night.

You look up into the sky and suddenly spot something bright zooming across the darkness.

It looks like a **star**, but it's moving fast.

Then the flash of bright light disappears.

You have just seen a **meteor** streaking across the night sky!

People sometimes call meteors shooting stars because they look like stars zooming across space. Meteors aren't really stars, though.

Space Rocks

The meteor you saw in the sky started out as a rocky space object called a **meteoroid**.

Meteoroids are small pieces that have broken away from **comets** or large space rocks called **asteroids**.

Most are tiny, like grains of sand, but some can be as large as 3 feet (1 m) wide.

When a meteoroid gets close to Earth, it flies into the **gases** surrounding our **planet**.

This layer of gases is called the **atmosphere**.

Once inside Earth's atmosphere, the meteoroid burns up and creates a bright streak of light.

Millions of meteoroids fly into Earth's atmosphere and burn up every day. Some are made of rock, while others are a mixture of rock and metal.

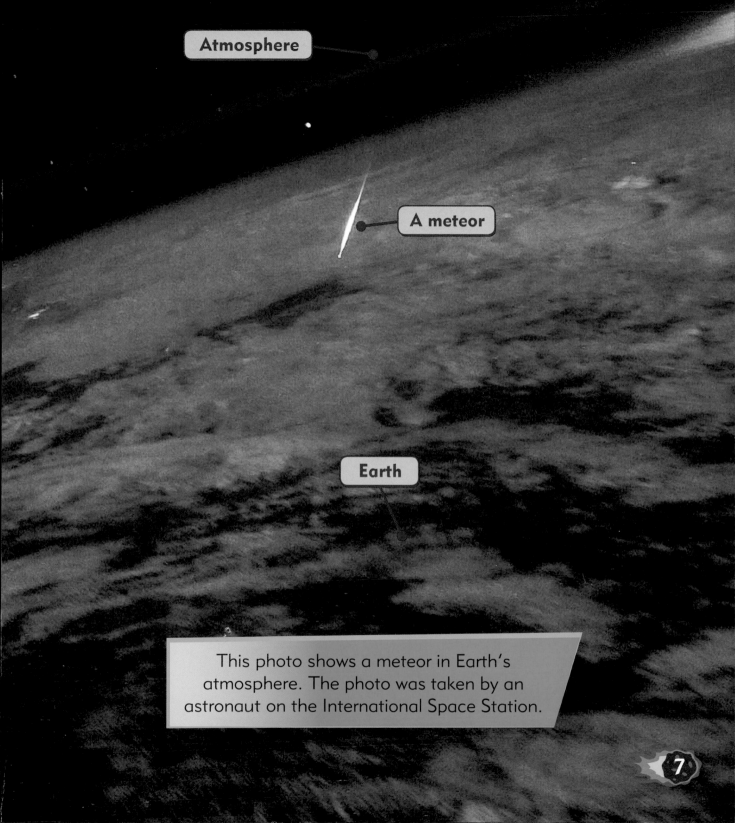

Atmosphere

A meteor

Earth

This photo shows a meteor in Earth's atmosphere. The photo was taken by an astronaut on the International Space Station.

The Solar System

Out in space, there are billions of meteoroids circling the Sun.

These small rocky chunks are joined by icy comets and asteroids.

There are also eight planets circling the Sun.

The planets are called Mercury, Venus, our home planet Earth, Mars, Jupiter, Saturn, Uranus, and Neptune.

The Sun and its family of space objects are called the **solar system**.

Most of the asteroids in the solar system are in a ring called the asteroid belt.

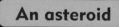

An asteroid

The Solar System

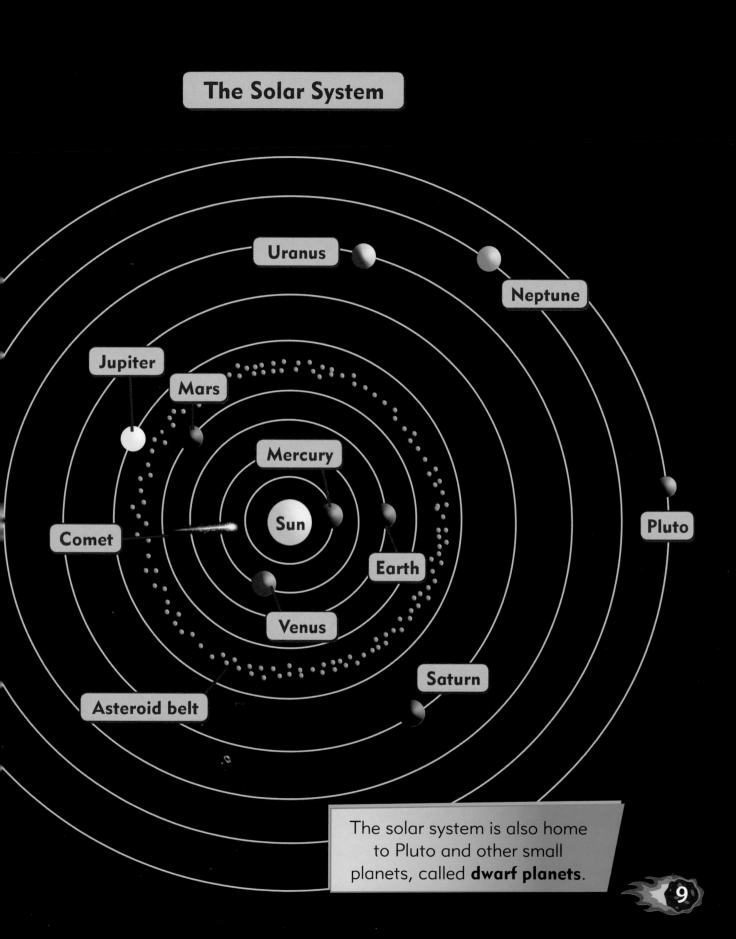

Uranus

Neptune

Jupiter

Mars

Mercury

Sun

Earth

Comet

Venus

Pluto

Saturn

Asteroid belt

The solar system is also home to Pluto and other small planets, called **dwarf planets**.

Asteroids

Most asteroids are shaped like lumpy potatoes.

They can be as small as a car or as large as a mountain.

There are millions of asteroids circling the Sun in the asteroid belt.

Sometimes these large space rocks crash into each other.

Smaller pieces break off and become meteoroids traveling through space.

Asteroids are made of rock mixed with metals. This asteroid is called Lutetia (loo-TEE-shee-yuh).

Meteoroid

Asteroid

This picture shows how an asteroid might look as it breaks into pieces. The small pieces are called meteoroids.

Asteroid Giants

The largest asteroid in the asteroid belt is named Ceres (SIHR-eez).

At 600 miles (966 km) across, it is almost as wide as Texas!

Vesta is also a gigantic asteroid that **orbits** the Sun in the asteroid belt.

At some time in the past, Vesta crashed into another large space object.

Dust, rocks, and mountain-sized chunks of the asteroid were thrown into space.

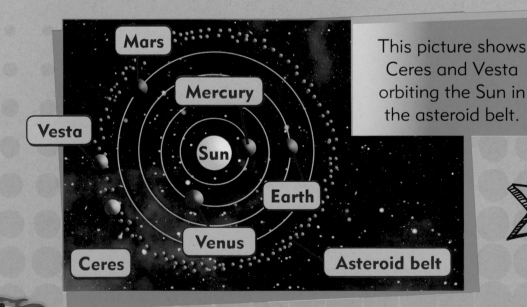

This picture shows Ceres and Vesta orbiting the Sun in the asteroid belt.

This picture shows the size of Ceres compared to Earth. Ceres is an asteroid and a dwarf planet.

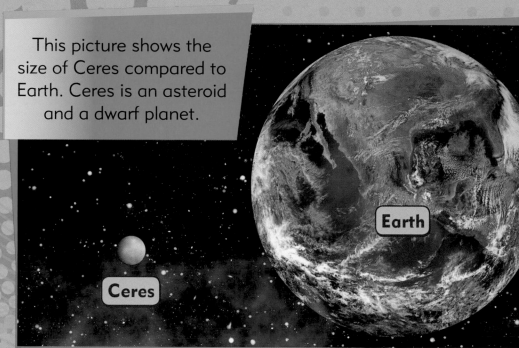

Ceres

Earth

Vesta

This is a photo of Vesta. It is just over 329 miles (530 km) wide. Scientists think that some pieces of Vesta have traveled through space and landed on Earth.

Meteorites

Sometimes, space objects that enter Earth's atmosphere do not completely burn up.

They may survive their fiery voyage and land on Earth.

A space object that lands on Earth is called a **meteorite**.

Meteorites may be chunks of rock or metal, or a mixture of both.

Some are just the size of a pebble, while others are basketball-sized or even larger.

Scientists have found several meteorites that they believe are pieces of the asteroid Vesta.

Scientists think this meteorite came from Vesta. It is about 4 inches (10 cm) wide.

The largest meteorite that's been found on Earth landed in Africa. It's called the Hoba meteorite. It is mostly made of iron and is as big as a car!

Hoba meteorite

This meteorite looks similar to a stone from here on Earth.

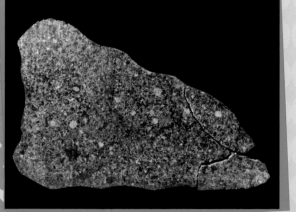

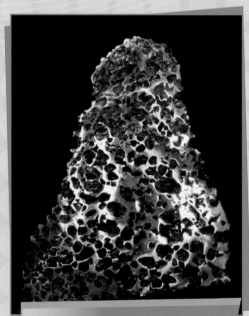

It's easy to see the metal in this meteorite.

Dangers from Space

Sometimes asteroids in the asteroid belt collide and get knocked outside of the belt.

Then they may begin circling the Sun in a pathway much closer to Earth.

In the past, large asteroids have collided with Earth.

Scientists keep watch on any large objects that are orbiting near our planet.

They can track the pathways these objects are taking and where they will go.

Today, scientists are sure that none of the asteroids they've discovered will collide with Earth.

Crater

This **crater** in Arizona is nearly a mile wide. It was made by a large space object that collided with Earth about 50,000 years ago.

Scientists found a giant crater near the town of Chicxulub (CHEEK-shuh-loob) in Mexico. It was made by a space object that was about 6 miles (10 km) wide. This object hit Earth 65 million years ago.

The space object that hit Mexico sent up huge clouds of hot ashes. It also caused earthquakes and made oceans flood the land. Many scientists believe this event helped kill off the dinosaurs and many other animals.

Giant Space Snowballs

Comets are large balls of ice mixed with rock and dust.

Most comets travel in a long, egg-shaped journey around the Sun.

When a comet is far from the Sun, it is a cold chunk of ice, dust, and rock.

As it gets closer to the Sun, it heats up.

Then it gives off a huge cloud of gases and dust.

The gases and dust form tails that stretch behind the comet for millions of miles.

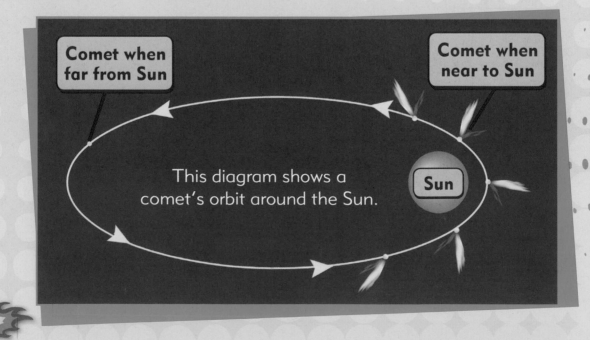

Comet when far from Sun

Comet when near to Sun

Sun

This diagram shows a comet's orbit around the Sun.

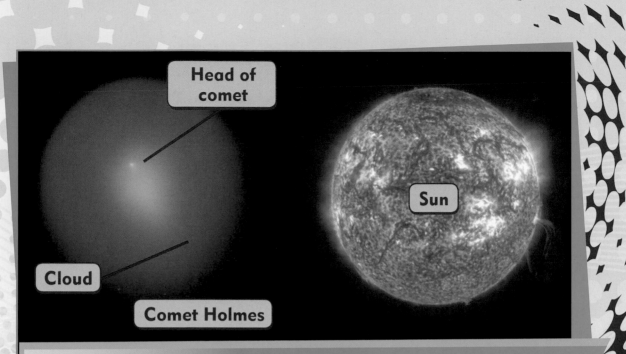

Head of comet

Cloud

Comet Holmes

Sun

This photo shows the gas and dust cloud around a comet called Comet Holmes. The cloud grew to be bigger than the Sun!

Comet

A comet seen from Earth. The head of a comet can be the size of a small town!

Tails of gas and dust

A comet seen through a telescope.

A Mission to a Comet

Scientists have sent space **probes** to study comets.

In 2014, a probe named *Rosetta* will fly around a comet deep in space.

Rosetta will release a smaller probe, which will land softly on the comet's surface.

This probe, called a lander, will study the comet and beam information back to Earth.

Rosetta will then follow the comet as it gets closer to the Sun and heats up.

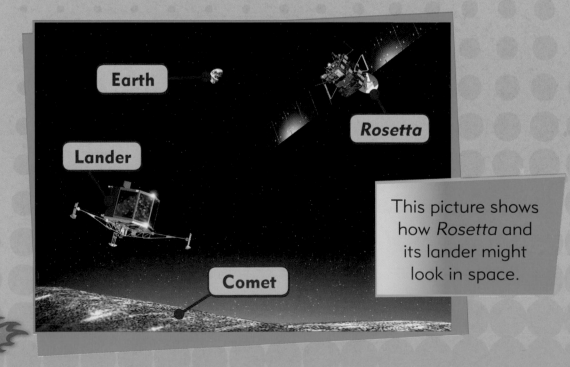

Earth

Rosetta

Lander

Comet

This picture shows how *Rosetta* and its lander might look in space.

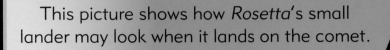

This picture shows how *Rosetta*'s small lander may look when it lands on the comet.

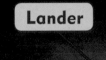

Lander

Surface of comet

Get Crafty
Comets and Asteroids Game

Invent your own board game all about comets, asteroids, and meteoroids.

Divide a large, square piece of construction paper into 25 squares. Draw or paint comets, asteroids, and meteoroids on the squares. Now make up the rules of your game, and play with a friend!

Game Ideas
Here are some ideas to get you started:

- Try throwing a dice and moving that number of squares. What happens when you land on a picture?
- Maybe you zoom 3 squares forward if you land on a comet?
- Perhaps you have to go back to the start if you land on an asteroid?

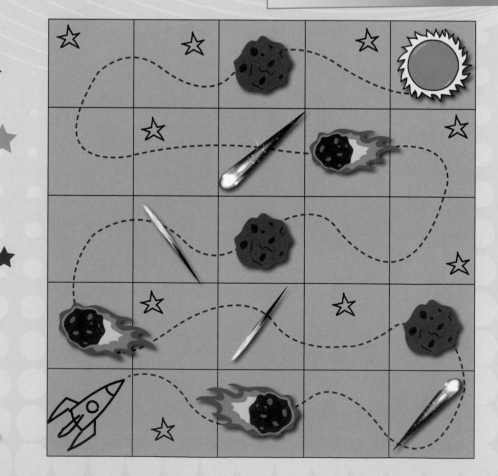

Glossary

asteroid (AS-teh-royd) A large rock that is orbiting the Sun. An asteroid can be as small as a car or bigger than a mountain.

atmosphere (AT-muh-sfeer) A layer of gases around a planet, moon, or star.

comet (KAH-mit) A space object made of ice, rock, and dust that is orbiting the Sun.

crater (KRAY-tur) A bowl-shaped hole in the ground. Craters are often caused by asteroids and other large, rocky objects hitting the surface of a planet or moon.

dwarf planet (DWARF PLAN-et) A round object in space that is orbiting the Sun. Dwarf planets are much smaller than the eight main planets.

gas (GASS) A substance, such as oxygen or helium, that does not have a definite shape or size.

meteor (MEE-tee-uhr) A small space object, such as a meteoroid, that appears as a steak of light as it burns up in Earth's atmosphere.

meteorite (MEE-tee-uhr-ite) A piece of another rocky object that has landed on a planet or a moon.

meteoroid (MEE-tee-uh-royd) A small piece of rock or dust that has broken free from a comet or asteroid.

orbit (OR-bit) To circle, or move around, another object.

planet (PLAN-et) A large object in space that is orbiting the Sun. Some planets, such as Earth, are made of rock. Others, such as Jupiter, are made of gases and liquids.

probe (PROBE) A spacecraft that does not have any people aboard. Probes are usually sent to planets or other objects in space to take photographs and collect information. They are controlled by scientists on Earth.

solar system (SOH-ler SIS-tem) The Sun and all the objects that orbit it, such as planets, their moons, asteroids, and comets.

star (STAR) A huge ball of burning gases in space. Our Sun is a star.

Index

Read More

Hughes, Catherine D. *First Big Book of Space (National Geographic Little Kids).* Washington, D.C.: The National Geographic Society (2012).

Rosa, Greg. *Comets and Asteroids: Space Rocks (Our Solar System).* New York: Gareth Stevens (2011).

Learn More Online

To learn more about comets, meteors, and asteroids, go to
www.rubytuesdaybooks.com/comet